Kitanai and Cavity Croc

BRUSH THEIR TEETH

by Thomas Kingsley Troupe

illustrated by Jamey Christoph

PICTURE WINDOW BOOKS
a capstone imprint

Kitanai the Origami Dog loved to jump and play around the pond. One day he leapt from lily pad to lily pad. He didn't want to fall into the water.

As he jumped across the pond,
a crocodile rose to the surface.

6

9

10

Whew! I hate to say it, but you've got alligator breath.

Is it bad?

It's not good. But brushing your tongue will help!

15

To make sure your teeth look and stay healthy, you should visit a dentist.

The dentist will check and clean your teeth and gums. The best part? You'll get a new toothbrush!

19

20

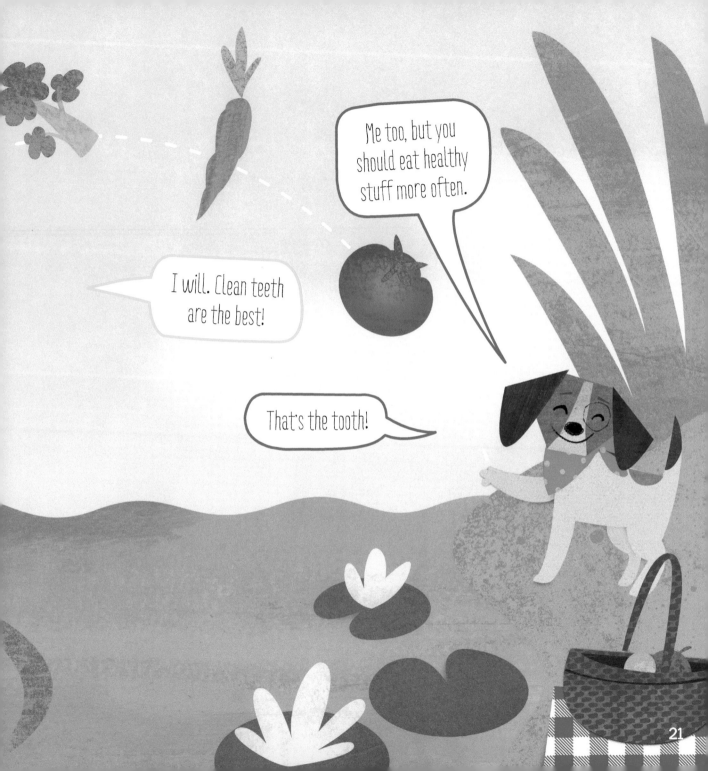

GLOSSARY

acid—a strong liquid that can break down teeth

bacteria—very small living things that exist all around you and inside you; some bacteria cause disease

decay—to break down or rot

gum—the firm flesh found at the base of a tooth

plaque—the coating of food, spit, and bacteria that forms on teeth and can cause them to break down

READ MORE

Huelin, Jodi. *A Cavity Is a Hole in Your Tooth.* Collins, N.Y.: Harper, 2010.

Rissman, Rebecca. *Should Billy Brush His Teeth: Taking Care of Yourself.* Chicago: Heinemann Library, 2013.

Tourville, Amanda Doering. *Brush, Floss, Rinse: Caring For Your Teeth and Gums.* Minneapolis: Picture Window Books, 2009.

INTERNET SITES

FactHound offers a safe, fun way to find Internet sites related to this book. All of the sites on FactHound have been researched by our staff.

Here's all you do:

Visit *www.facthound.com*

Type in this code: 9781479560806

Super-cool stuff! Check out projects, games and lots more at **www.capstonekids.com**

INDEX

Editor: Jeni Wittrock
Designer: Ashlee Suker
Art Director: Nathan Gassman
Production Specialist: Laura Manthe
The illustrations in this book were created digitally.

Picture Window Books are published by Capstone,
1710 Roe Crest Drive, North Mankato, Minnesota 56003
www.capstonepub.com

Library of Congress Cataloging-in-Publication
Troupe, Thomas Kingsley.
Kitanai and Cavity Croc brush their teeth/by Thomas
Kingsley Troupe.
pages cm.—(Nonfiction Picture Books. Kitanai's Healthy Habits)
Summary: "Kitanai the dog teaches Cavity Croc how to keep teeth
clean"—Provided by publisher.
Audience: Ages 5–7
Audience: K to grade 3
ISBN 978-1-4795-6116-2 (eBook pdf)
ISBN 978-1-4795-6080-6 (library binding)
ISBN 978-1-4795-6112-4 (paperback)
1. Teeth—Care and hygiene—Juvenile literature. I. Title.
RK63.T76 2015
617.60083—dc23
2014021102

Other titles in this series:

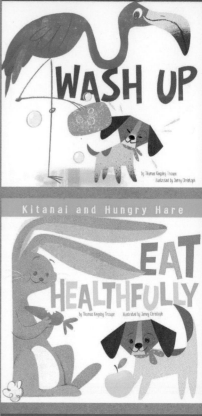